Contents

Leveled Reading: Social Studies, SV 9781419099656

Features

The *Leveled Reading* series uses a variety of carefully leveled passages within a specific genre to supplement learning. In this way, the needs of the variety of readers in the classroom are met.

The high-interest passages within the series may be used for whole group or small group instruction as well as for independent practice. If used for independent practice, passages should be selected at the student's independent reading level to ensure success. For instances where the student will receive direct support, the passages should be at the student's instructional level. It is important that the key vocabulary within passages be overviewed with the student and that the student be encouraged to utilize strategies for understanding new and unfamiliar words.

Each book within the series is divided into lessons. The lessons follow a similar format to help improve the student's reading, fluency, comprehension, vocabulary, and critical thinking. Each lesson includes a leveled passage, Reading Comprehension Check, Vocabulary Practice, and Critical Thinking Activity.

Leveled passages open with a **Get Ready to Read** section that connects the student to the text. The student should read the passage once for pleasure and then a second time for understanding, noting the boldface vocabulary words. The student may write brief summaries or comments about the text in the margins to document his or her understanding of the text. The student should additionally read sections of the text aloud to continue to build his or her fluency skills.

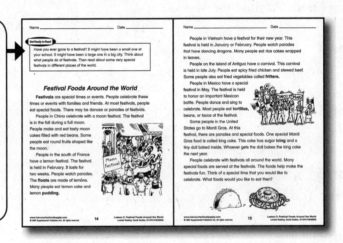

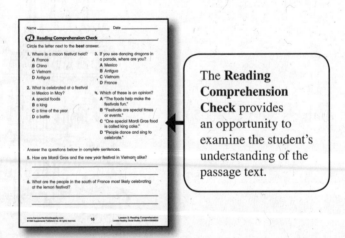

The **Reading Comprehension Check** provides an opportunity to examine the student's understanding of the passage text.

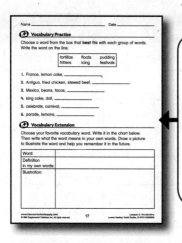

The **Vocabulary Practice** page allows the student to practice his or her knowledge of the key words from the passage. In addition, most vocabulary pages include a **Vocabulary Extension,** where the student may apply higher-order thinking skills to the newly acquired vocabulary.

The **Critical Thinking Activity** involves the student in the process of conceptualizing, applying, analyzing, synthesizing, and/or evaluating information related to the passage.

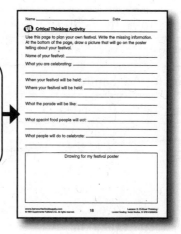

Page 4 features a helpful **Passage Titles and Levels Chart** for easy reference, and page 5 consists of a **Series Scope and Sequence Chart** that lists the page numbers where specific skills are utilized within the four-book series.

Pages 90–93 are graphic organizers. Some Critical Thinking Activity pages utilize these graphic organizers; however, the graphic organizers may also be utilized as pre- or post-reading activities to additionally support reading of the passages.

An answer key is found on pages 94–96.

Passage Title	Grade Level	F&P Level	DRA Level
Around the Neighborhood	K–1	E	10
In Outer Space	1	G	16
Festival Foods Around the World	1–2	H	20
Arctic Life	1–2	I	20
Castles	1–2	I	28
Amazing Trains	2	L	28
Corn: A Native American Gift	2	M	28
Farm Life Long Ago	2	L	18
Laura Ingalls Wilder: An Author's Story	2–3	L	38
Cities Around the World	2–3	M	34
Explorers: Searching for Adventure	2–3	M	38
The Perseverance of Charles F. Bolden, Jr.	3–4	Q	40
The U.S. President	4–5	V	50

Levels in this chart are subjective. Educators are encouraged to freely adjust designated levels according to their personal evaluation.

Grade Level represents the grade level at which the text is written and the level at which the student is reading.

F&P Level = Fountas and Pinnell Guided Reading Level
Matching Books to Readers, Using Leveled Books in Guided Reading K–3.
Irene C. Fountas and Gay Su Pinnell. Heinemann, 1999.
Guiding Readers and Writers 3–6. Irene C. Fountas and Gay Su Pinnell.
Heinemann, 2001.

DRA Level = Developmental Reading Assessment Level
Developmental Reading Assessment Resource Guide.
Joetta Beaver, Celebration Press, 1997.

Series Scope and Sequence Chart

Reading Skills	Science	Social Studies	Realistic Fiction	Tales
COMPREHENSION				
Literal Comprehension				
Understanding Facts and Details	7, 11, 16, 21, 26, 31, 37, 39, 44, 52, 60, 69, 78, 80, 87	7, 11, 16, 21, 27, 34, 72, 80, 87	7, 12, 17, 22, 27, 32, 38, 44, 59, 68, 73, 82	22, 69
Identifying Plot			7, 22, 24, 34, 38, 44, 46, 59, 61, 73	7, 11, 16, 28, 30, 43, 45, 51, 69, 77, 86
Identifying Main Idea and Supporting Details	7, 11, 16, 21, 26, 31, 37, 44, 52, 60, 69, 78, 87	7, 11, 21, 27, 34, 41, 43, 47, 63, 72, 89	12, 27, 52	28, 60, 77
Summarizing	23, 27, 37, 61, 78, 80	47, 87	38, 82	30, 43
Interpretive Skills				
Retelling	9, 33, 39, 70, 79, 87	56	17, 24, 87	77
Distinguishing Fact from Opinion	7, 31, 54, 78	16, 87	59	
Sequencing	18, 69	34, 36, 49, 74	7, 12, 29, 34, 40, 44, 68, 73, 78, 87	7, 61, 77
Identifying Cause and Effect	37, 54, 60, 89	23, 41	12, 22, 52, 69, 73, 87	35, 51, 53, 69, 86, 88
Recognizing Setting			32, 46, 61	35, 45, 61, 86
Comparing and Contrasting	16, 33, 44, 62	9, 16, 21, 27, 47, 56, 63, 72	52, 54, 78	18, 22, 35, 43, 51, 77, 86
Interpreting Text Features		41, 63		11
Critical Thinking				
Categorizing and Classifying	21, 33	17, 87	38	
Creative Response	9, 13, 18, 23, 28, 89	9, 13, 18, 29, 36, 43, 49, 65, 74	9, 14, 19, 24, 40, 46, 54, 61, 69, 78, 87	9, 13, 37, 45, 53, 71
Understanding Realism and Fantasy	23, 46		32, 38, 73	11, 16, 22, 28, 51
Making Predictions	39		7, 27	11, 28
Drawing Conclusions	7, 11, 26, 28, 38, 52, 54, 69, 78, 79	16, 27, 47, 54, 63	22, 38, 52, 53, 68, 82	9, 13, 45, 53
Identifying Author's Purpose	7, 11, 16, 21, 28, 44, 54, 62, 69, 78	11, 21, 41, 80	12, 68, 82	16, 35, 43
Analyzing Character		54	7, 12, 22, 24, 27, 28, 38, 52, 54, 73, 78, 87	7, 11, 22, 28, 30, 35, 43, 51, 60, 62, 69, 77, 86, 88
Making Inferences	7, 13, 16, 21, 27, 31, 38, 60	7, 16, 21, 27, 41, 47, 54	27, 32, 44, 73	16, 28, 43, 51, 61, 69
Making Judgments	33, 39, 46, 70	23, 80, 89		13, 35
Identifying Theme			87	16, 22, 69, 79, 86
Identifying Genre		54, 80		16, 28, 35, 69
Application of Newly Acquired Knowledge	13, 18, 23, 32, 37, 44, 46, 54, 61, 62, 69, 71, 80, 87, 89	13, 23, 29, 36, 43, 49, 65, 74	9, 19, 34, 40, 69, 78	9, 24
VOCABULARY				
Naming Words				23, 70
Rhyming Words	32, 38, 70	28	8, 60	8, 17, 23
Classifying	37	17	23, 28, 45, 53	29
Context Clues	8, 12, 17, 22, 27, 31, 32, 38, 45, 53, 61, 70, 79	8, 12, 22, 28, 35, 48, 55, 64, 81, 88	8, 13, 23, 33, 39, 45, 53, 60, 67, 77, 86	8, 12, 17, 23, 29, 44, 52, 61, 70, 78, 87
Synonyms	22, 32, 38, 45, 53, 79, 88	35	13, 18, 28, 60, 77, 86	29, 70
Antonyms	17, 32, 70	12, 22, 28, 81	60, 86	8, 29, 70, 78
Words with Multiple Meanings		88	8, 18, 39	17, 23, 61, 70, 78
Prefixes			13	78
Suffixes			13, 86	17, 23, 44
Phonics	32, 70	12		
Compound Words		28, 81	13, 23, 33	61

Name _____   Date _____

When you step outside your door, you step into your neighborhood.
Read about one child's neighborhood. Are the same kinds of places in
your own neighborhood?

Around the Neighborhood

My **neighborhood** is a busy place.

There is a lot to do.

There is a park.

I can run and play there.

There is a **supermarket.**

I can buy food there.

There is a **bakery.**

I can get a snack there.

There is a post office.

I can mail a letter there.

There is a **library.**

I can find many books there.

My neighborhood is a busy place.

How is your neighborhood like mine?

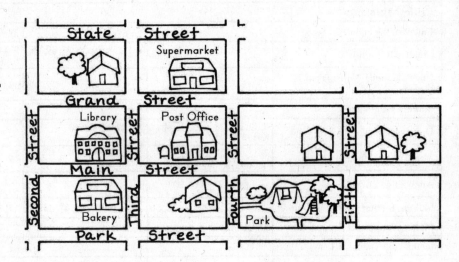

Name _____ Date _____

Complete each sentence below. Use what you read in the passage.

1. The neighborhood in the passage is a busy place because _____

_____.

2. Two places to buy food in a neighborhood are _____

_____.

3. You can buy stamps for a letter at _____

_____.

4. You can run races in _____

_____.

5. If you want to find something to read, you can go to _____

_____.

6. If you are hungry, you can _____

_____.

7. You can play games at _____

_____.

8. The main idea of this passage is that _____

_____.

Name _____ Date _____

 Vocabulary Practice

Circle the letter next to the **best** answer.

1. In this passage, *bakery* means—
   A a place to eat supper.
   B a place to buy freshly baked bread.
   C a person who bakes bread.
   D a store where fruit is sold.

2. In this passage, *neighborhood* means—
   A all the places close to your house.
   B a place that is always busy.
   C a part of a city without buildings.
   D a place where people buy and sell things.

3. In this passage, *library* means a place where you—
   A buy books.
   B go to school.
   C check out books.
   D play with friends.

4. In this passage, *supermarket* means—
   A a place where people sit down and eat supper.
   B an indoor place where children can play.
   C an outdoor place where people buy things.
   D a place where many kinds of foods are sold.

 Vocabulary Extension

Use a vocabulary word in a fun way! Draw a picture to go with each sentence.

Good smells come from the **bakery.**	We bought milk at the **supermarket.**

Name _____   Date _____

In the space below, draw a map of your neighborhood. Write the name of each place.

I.

My Neighborhood

Answer the questions below in complete sentences.

2. How is your neighborhood like the neighborhood in the passage?

_____

_____

3. How is your neighborhood different from the neighborhood in the passage?

_____

_____

Name _____ Date _____

Get Ready to Read

At night when you look up at the sky, you see the darkness of outer space. You may also see Earth's moon, a few planets, and many stars. Read about the people who study outer space and travel there.

In Outer Space

Planets and moons are in outer space. **Scientists** use **telescopes** to see them. **Satellites** travel into space to send us **photos** of **distant** planets.

Astronauts work in outer space. It takes many years of training to be an astronaut. They learn how to float in space. They practice spacewalking underwater. Astronauts eat special foods in space. They also wear special spacesuits.

Alan Shepard was the first person from the United States in space. John Glenn was the first U.S. astronaut to **orbit** Earth. Neil Armstrong was the first person to walk on the moon. He placed the U.S. flag on the moon. Sally Ride was the first woman from the United States in space. Roberta Bondar was the first Canadian woman in space.

Someday you might travel in outer space.

Name _____ Date _____

✔ Reading Comprehension Check

Circle the letter next to the **best** answer.

1. A satellite is used to—
   A look at planets that are underwater.
   B take photos of things in outer space.
   C travel into outer space.
   D train astronauts for outer space.

2. According to the passage, what do astronauts do in outer space?
   A float
   B go underwater
   C sell telescopes
   D watch movies

3. What does an astronaut use a lot in outer space?
   A a telescope
   B a flag
   C a satellite
   D a special suit

4. Who was the first U.S. astronaut to travel in space?
   A Sally Ride
   B John Glenn
   C Neil Armstrong
   D Alan Shepard

5. This passage is mostly about—
   A planets.
   B scientists.
   C outer space.
   D spacesuits.

6. The author most likely wrote this passage to—
   A give information about outer space.
   B tell about one astronaut.
   C make readers want to take pictures of outer space.
   D tell what scientists do.

Answer the question in complete sentences.

7. Why does the author tell about Roberta Bondar?

_____

_____

Name _____ Date _____

 Vocabulary Practice

Write the vocabulary word from the box that fits each clue to finish the puzzle.

| telescope | photos | scientists | distant |
| astronauts | satellites | orbit | |

Across

1. These things send pictures of planets to Earth.
3. This can be used to look at things that are far away.
6. to go around a planet or moon
7. They study moons and planets.

Down

2. These people travel to outer space.
4. the opposite of *near*
5. This word and the word *food* begin with the same sound.

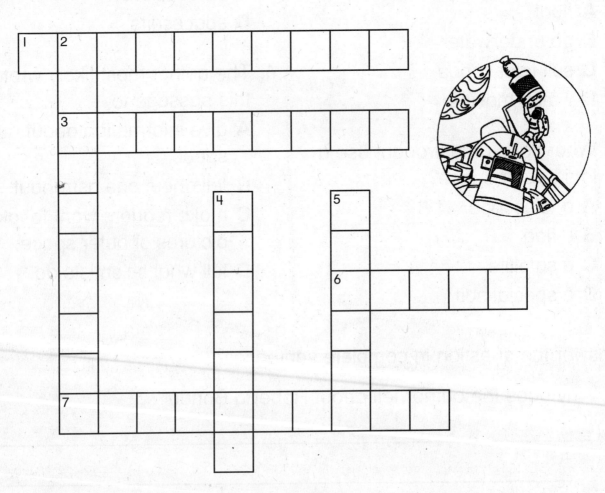

Name _____ Date _____

 Critical Thinking Activity

Imagine that first you are in training to be an astronaut and then you go on a trip to outer space. On the page in your diary for March 14, write about what training is like. On the page for July 20, write about what it is like to be in outer space. Use what you learned in the passage, as well as your own ideas.

March 14

July 20

EXTRA: Find a photograph of Earth as it looks to astronauts who are in outer space. When you write in your diary for July 20, describe what Earth looks like.

Name _____ Date _____

Have you ever gone to a festival? It might have been a small one at your school. It might have been a large one in a big city. Think about what people do at festivals. Then read about some very special festivals in different places of the world.

Festival Foods Around the World

Festivals are special times or events. People celebrate these times or events with families and friends. At most festivals, people eat special foods. There may be dances or parades at festivals.

People in China celebrate with a moon festival. The festival is in the fall during a full moon. People make and eat tasty moon cakes filled with red beans. Some people eat round fruits shaped like the moon.

People in the south of France have a lemon festival. The festival is held in February. It lasts for two weeks. People watch parades. The **floats** are made of lemons. Many people eat lemon cake and lemon **pudding.**

People in Vietnam have a festival for their new year. This festival is held in January or February. People watch parades that have dancing dragons. Many people eat rice cakes wrapped in leaves.

People on the island of Antigua have a carnival. This carnival is held in late July. People eat spicy fried chicken and stewed beef. Some people also eat fried vegetables called **fritters.**

People in Mexico have a special festival in May. The festival is held to honor an important Mexican battle. People dance and sing to celebrate. Most people eat **tortillas,** beans, or tacos at the festival.

Some people in the United States go to Mardi Gras. At this festival, there are parades and special foods. One special Mardi Gras food is called king cake. This cake has sugar **icing** and a tiny doll baked inside. Whoever gets the doll bakes the king cake the next year.

People celebrate with festivals all around the world. Many special foods are served at the festivals. The foods help make the festivals fun. Think of a special time that you would like to celebrate. What foods would you like to eat then?

Leveled Reading: Social Studies, SV 9781419099656

Name _____ Date _____

 Reading Comprehension Check

Circle the letter next to the **best** answer.

1. Where is a moon festival held?
   - A France
   - B China
   - C Vietnam
   - D Antigua

2. What is celebrated at a festival in Mexico in May?
   - A special foods
   - B a king
   - C a time of the year
   - D a battle

3. If you see dancing dragons in a parade, where are you?
   - A Mexico
   - B Antigua
   - C Vietnam
   - D France

4. Which of these is an opinion?
   - A "The foods help make the festivals fun."
   - B "Festivals are special times or events."
   - C "One special Mardi Gras food is called king cake."
   - D "People dance and sing to celebrate."

Answer the questions below in complete sentences.

5. How are Mardi Gras and the new year festival in Vietnam alike?

_____

_____

6. What are the people in the south of France most likely celebrating at the lemon festival?

_____

_____

Leveled Reading: Social Studies, SV 9781419099656

Name _____ Date _____

 Vocabulary Practice

Choose a word from the box that **best** fits with each group of words.
Write the word on the line.

tortillas	floats	pudding
fritters	icing	festivals

1. France, lemon cake, _____

2. Antigua, fried chicken, stewed beef, _____

3. Mexico, beans, tacos, _____

4. king cake, doll, _____

5. celebrate, carnival, _____

6. parade, lemons, _____

Vocabulary Extension

Choose your favorite vocabulary word. Write it in the chart below.
Then write what the word means in your own words. Draw a picture
to illustrate the word and help you remember it in the future.

Word:	
Definition in my own words:	
Illustration:	

Name _____ Date _____

 ## Critical Thinking Activity

Use this page to plan your own festival. Write the missing information. At the bottom of the page, draw a picture that will go on the poster telling about your festival.

Name of your festival: _____

What you are celebrating: _____

_____

When your festival will be held: _____

Where your festival will be held: _____

_____

What the parade will be like: _____

_____

What special food people will eat: _____

_____

What people will do to celebrate: _____

_____

```
                        Drawing for my festival poster




```

Name _____ Date _____

The part of our planet that is as far north as you can go is a very cold place most of the time. You may think this place is so cold that nothing can live there. But that isn't true! Read to learn about animals and people who live in this cold place.

Arctic Life

Do you know of any places that are very cold? One cold place has lots of snow and ice. It is home to polar bears. The North Pole is also there. What is this part of the world? It is the Arctic!

Many kinds of animals live in the Arctic. Arctic foxes and Arctic hares live on land. These animals have white fur in winter. Their thick fur keeps them warm. Reindeer also live in the Arctic. Their large hooves help them walk on snow.

Leveled Reading: Social Studies, SV 9781419099656

Seals and walruses swim in the Arctic Ocean. Sometimes they climb onto the land or ice. A thick **layer** of fat keeps these animals warm. The fat is called **blubber.** The Arctic also has many kinds of birds. It even has its own kind of bumblebee.

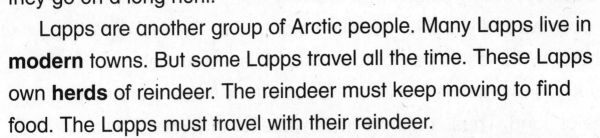

People live in the Arctic, too. The Inuit are one group of Arctic people. Most Inuit live in houses with plenty of heat. They shop in stores for clothes and food. But some Inuit still hunt for food. They build **igloos** when they go on a long hunt.

Lapps are another group of Arctic people. Many Lapps live in **modern** towns. But some Lapps travel all the time. These Lapps own **herds** of reindeer. The reindeer must keep moving to find food. The Lapps must travel with their reindeer.

Winter in the Arctic is very **harsh.** Snow covers all the land. Ice covers the Arctic Ocean. It gets so cold that a person's breath freezes! In some places the sun never rises. The sky is dark all day and all night.

In summer some parts of the Arctic stay snowy. But in other parts the snow **melts.** Plants grow, and flowers bloom. Baby animals are born. In some places the sun never sets. The sky is bright all day and night.

The Arctic is a land of snow and polar bears. It is a land of plants and flowers. It is a land of the Inuit and the Lapps. It is a home for animals, plants, and people.

Name _____ Date _____

✓ Reading Comprehension Check

Answer each question in complete sentences.

1. How does blubber help seals and walruses in the Arctic?

_____

_____

2. How are summer and winter different in the Arctic?

_____

_____

3. How are Lapps and Inuit alike?

_____

_____

4. Why do you think Arctic hares have white fur?

_____

_____

_____

5. Why did the author most likely write the passage?

_____

_____

6. What is the main idea of the passage?

_____

_____

Name _____ Date _____

 Vocabulary Practice

Choose a word from the box to complete each sentence. Write each word on the line.

herds	modern	melts	layer
harsh	blubber	igloos	

1. The opposite of *freezes* is _____.

2. Groups of animals are called _____.

3. Inuit sometimes use blocks of ice to build houses that are called

   _____.

4. The opposite of *old-time* is _____.

5. A layer of fat on animals living in cold places is called

   _____.

6. In a _____ winter, the weather is very bad.

7. A _____ is one thickness of something over or under another thickness.

 Vocabulary Extension

Choose two vocabulary words. Describe something that is an example and something that is not an example for each word.

Word:	Word:
Example:	Example:
Non-example:	Non-example:

Name _____ Date _____

 Critical Thinking Activity

Part 1 Complete the chart. Use information you learned in the passage. You do not have to write complete sentences.

EFFECT	CAUSE
1. _____ _____	Thick fur
Walruses and seals stay warm in the cold ocean.	2. _____ _____
3. _____ _____	Large hooves
Some Lapps move around all the time.	4. _____ _____
In winter the sky is dark all day and all night.	5. _____ _____

Part 2 Circle *winter* or *summer* and then complete the sentence.

I would rather travel in the Arctic in the **winter** **summer** because

_____

_____

_____.

Name _____ Date _____

You most likely have read stories or fairy tales about people who lived in a castle. What do you remember about the castle? Have you ever wondered what it would be like to live in one? In this passage, you will learn about castles of long ago.

Castles

Most castles were built hundreds of years ago. Many kings and queens had castles built. They wanted to protect the people they ruled. They also wanted to protect their land.

Many castles were built on low ground. People living in them could come and go easily. Some castles were built on hills or by rivers. **Enemies** had a hard time getting to castles on hills or by rivers.

The first castles were made of wood and dirt. They were easy for enemies to burn. Later castles were made of stone. Building with stone took many, many workers.

Castle walls were very tall. A tall wall was hard for an enemy to climb. Castle walls were thick, too. People could walk on top of the thick walls.

Some castle walls had **towers** along them. People often lived in the towers. Some castles had **moats** around them. A moat was a deep ditch filled with water.

A castle with a moat also had a **drawbridge.** The drawbridge was a bridge over the moat. People could raise the drawbridge. Then enemies could not get across the moat.

Inside the castle walls was a big **courtyard.** Hay and firewood were stored there. People worked in the courtyard, too. They made tools and chopped wood.

The people of the castle needed a lot of food. Many castles had gardens. People grew some plants to eat. People grew other plants because they were pretty.

Most castles had a large room called a great hall. **Feasts** were held in the great hall. These large meals went on for hours. People ate geese, eels, pies, and puddings.

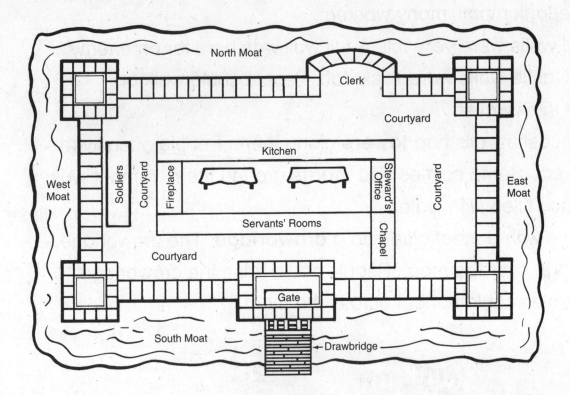

The kitchen of a castle was a busy place. Cooks worked at big tables to make foods. They baked bread in a stone oven. They cooked meat over an open fire.

A king and his family often had their own tower. It often stood at the center of the castle. The tower had bedrooms and a living room. But it did not have closets.

Today many castles are museums. Visitors climb towers, explore rooms, and think about the people who once lived there.

Name _____   Date _____

Circle the letter next to the **best** answer.

1. Why did kings and queens build castles?
   A to have a place to live
   B to keep people and land safe
   C to be able to see far away
   D to hide from their enemies

2. What made the first castles different from later castles?
   A what they were made of
   B how big they were
   C where they were built
   D who lived in them

3. From this passage, you can tell that—
   A most castles were built long ago.
   B all castles were very large.
   C only ten castles had moats and drawbridges.
   D all castles were built by kings and queens.

4. What is the first page of the passage mostly about?
   A when castles were built
   B the people who lived in castles
   C castle walls
   D building castles

5. Which of these did NOT make a castle safer?
   A building a moat around it
   B building a great hall in it
   C building it on a hill
   D building it by a river

6. Castles built on low ground—
   A were built earlier than castles built on hills.
   B were often burned by enemies.
   C were not as safe as castles built on hills.
   D were almost always made of wood.

Name _____ Date _____

 Vocabulary Practice

Write the vocabulary word from the box that fits each clue to finish the puzzle.

feasts	enemies	courtyards	moats
drawbridges	museums	towers	

Across

3. a compound word that describes places inside castle walls

5. rhymes with *hours;* people lived in them

6. means the opposite of *friends*

7. rhymes with *beasts;* means "large meals"

Down

1. rhymes with *floats;* they were filled with water

2. a compound word that describes things that helped protect castles

4. places where people see things from the past

Lesson 5: Vocabulary
Leveled Reading: Social Studies, SV 9781419099656

Name _____ Date _____

Draw a picture of a castle you would like to live in. Remember to draw things that will help to protect your castle from enemies! Label all the parts of your castle. Then describe it on the lines below your drawing.

My Castle

_____

_____

_____

_____

_____

EXTRA: Find a picture or a photograph of a castle in a book or on the Internet. How is it like your castle? How is it different? Use a copy of the Compare and Contrast Chart on page 92 to show your answers.

Name _____ Date _____

When you hear a train whistle or see a train pass by, do you ever wish you could be on that train? Do you ever think about how long trains have been around? Do you ever wonder if there are trains that are really different from the ones you've heard or seen? In this passage, you'll learn a lot about trains—from the first slow trains to the newest trains that are very, very fast.

Amazing Trains

Trains are an important way to move people and goods. Some take people to work. Others ship food to market. Some **haul** steel to **factories.**

Today trains move with amazing speed. They are pulled by strong engines. But the first trains were wagons pulled by horses. They moved very slowly.

Then engines were built to pull trains. The first engines used steam to move trains along tracks. The trains were mostly used to move goods. They could move as fast as horses.

The first steam trains to carry people were in England. People sat in open cars on these trains. Each car looked like a stagecoach. These trains were the fastest way to travel.

Steam trains moved things quickly. Their engines were called **locomotives.** *Locomotion* means "to move from place to place." A steam locomotive could pull a train with many cars.

Soon there were also steam trains in the United States. A steam train named the "Tom Thumb" raced a horse and lost. After that, trains were built to move faster.

Many tracks were built across the United States. One railroad company built tracks from east to west. Another built tracks from west to east. The companies celebrated when the two sets of tracks met. The companies **pounded** a gold spike into the rails. This joined the tracks together. Then trains could travel from coast to coast. A train trip from New York to California would take only one week. The trip would take six months by horse!

People began to take more train trips. They met at the train station in town. A conductor helped them into the cars. People sat together in rows. Most cars had roofs and open windows.

It took a lot of work to keep the trains moving from town to town. Some workers built the railroad tracks. Others kept the trains running well. The engineers kept the trains going full speed ahead.

Soon better cars were built for trains that carried people. George Pullman helped build sleeping cars. They gave people a place to rest. Then people could take longer train trips.

Trains were also used to move people in cities. Rail lines were built underground in tunnels and high above the ground. In this way, the trains, known as subway trains, could go faster. Subway trains made it easier and quicker for people to travel within a city and the areas around it. Many people used subway trains to get to and from work.

Engines were built to pull more cars and carry more people. Engines were also made to move even faster. Soon trains could move mail, people, or food in a short time.

People began to think of better ways to move people on trains. They began to think of faster trains to move people.

High-speed trains were invented. These trains were built to move at speeds of 125 miles per hour or more. The first high-speed train was in Japan. It was called the bullet train because it looked like a bullet. Other countries such as France, Germany, and Spain also built high-speed rail lines. Some people took high-speed trains instead of driving. Some people rode these trains instead of airplanes for long trips.

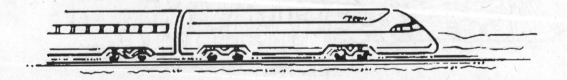

Name _____ Date _____

A rail line was also built underwater between England and France. This underwater rail tunnel was called The Channel Tunnel. It was 31 miles long and about 150 feet deep. People and goods could travel between England and France much more quickly. Today a high-speed rail line runs through the tunnel. Travel is even faster!

Today there are even faster high-speed trains. The bullet trains speed along at over 280 miles per hour. Trains in Japan called maglev trains have been tested at 360 miles per hour.

Trains are changing all the time. They are being built to move faster than ever. They are being built to carry more and to give a smoother ride. What do you think trains will be like in the future?

Name _____ Date _____

✓ Reading Comprehension Check

Complete each sentence below.

1. Before there were trains pulled by engines, trains were _____

_____

_____.

2. People in England _____

_____

before people in the United States did.

3. Two railroad companies in the United States wanted trains to be

able to _____

_____

_____.

4. Four kinds of workers worked on the trains or on the railroad tracks.

They were _____

_____

_____.

5. Before sleeping cars were built, _____

_____

_____.

6. Today trains are used to _____

_____

_____.

Leveled Reading: Social Studies, SV 9781419099656

Name _____ Date _____

 Vocabulary Practice

Read each sentence. Circle the letter next to the **best** meaning for the underlined word.

1. Trains <u>haul</u> goods from one place to another.
   A sell
   B mail
   C walk
   D carry

2. In <u>factories</u>, steel is changed into things like railroad tracks.
   A buildings where people and machines make things
   B places where people change trains
   C towns where people work
   D places where conductors work on trains

3. The man <u>pounded</u> the spike.
   A looked at
   B paid for
   C hit
   D tested

4. The <u>locomotive</u> arrived late.
   A engineer
   B conductor
   C steam engine
   D stagecoach

 Vocabulary Extension

Choose your favorite vocabulary word. Complete the graphic organizer.

Word:	
Looks like:	
Sounds like:	
Feels like:	
Synonym:	

Name _____ Date _____

 Critical Thinking Activity

1. Imagine that you can travel back in time. Write in your diary about a train trip you took in England in 1825. This was the year that the first steam train carried people sitting in open cars. Use what you learned in the passage, as well as your own ideas.

> November 10, 1825
>
> _____
> _____
> _____
> _____

2. Next write in your diary about a train trip you took in the United States in 1875. You traveled for two days and slept in a sleeping car. Use what you learned in the passage, as well as your own ideas.

> May 6, 1875
>
> _____
> _____
> _____
> _____

3. Finally write in your diary about a train trip you took in Japan in 2003. You made a quick trip between two cities. Use what you learned in the passage, as well as your own ideas.

> July 22, 2003
>
> _____
> _____
> _____
> _____

4. Use a copy of the Sequence Chain on page 91 to show how train travel for people has changed. Start with the first steam trains that carried people and end with bullet trains.

Name _____ Date _____

Get Ready to Read

Almost everyone has eaten corn in one way or another. It may have been roasted corn on the cob. It may have been corn that was dried, ground up, and used to make corn bread. Do you ever think about how corn grows? Do you ever wonder how long people have been growing it? In this passage, you're going to find out!

Corn: A Native American Gift

How did corn first begin to grow? Some Native American **legends** from long ago attempt to explain it.

One legend tells about three sisters named Corn, Beans, and Squash. Corn was the oldest sister. She had yellow hair and stood very tall. Everywhere she walked, corn plants grew in her footprints.

No one knows for certain how corn first began to grow, but it has been grown for thousands of years. The oldest corncob fossil was found in Mexico. It is about 7,000 years old!

The Native Americans who lived in Mexico learned to plant corn and help it grow. Often it was the only food they had to eat. They called it **maize.** Maize means "bread of life."

Native Americans learned to use all the parts of the corn plant. They used the leaves to make baskets, beds, and shoes. They even used the **stalks** to make roofs for houses. Soon items made from the corn plant were used as money for trade.

Then the Pilgrims came to North America. Native Americans shared corn with them. They taught the Pilgrims how to plant and grow corn, and they showed the Pilgrims that it could be used many ways.

An Important Crop

Today farmers all around the world grow corn. It can grow in both warm and cold climates. Corn is an important **crop** in North America, China, France, Russia, and India.

More corn is grown in the United States than in any other country. The area where it is grown is called the Corn Belt.

Corn takes about four to six months to grow. It is usually planted in the spring. After a seed is planted, it takes about two months for the plant to grow into a strong cornstalk.

Soon buds appear on each stalk. These buds take about two months to become fully grown ears of corn. Then the ears are ready to be pulled off the stalk.

Some corn is left on the stalk a month after it is ripe. It dries and turns brown. Then the dry, hard corn can be used as food for animals. Farmers use this corn to feed cattle, hogs, chickens, and sheep.

The core of an ear of corn is the **cob.** It holds rows of corn **kernels.** They are the small parts on the cob, and they look like teeth. Some kernels are soft, and others are hard. Kernels can be blue, black, white, orange, red, or yellow.

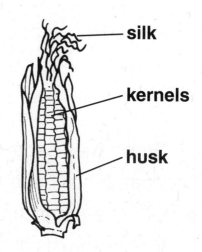

Corn **husks** are the tough leaves that grow around an ear of corn. They protect the kernels from insects and bad weather. Corn **silk** grows inside the husks with the kernels. Corn silk is soft and stringy.

A Tasty Food

There are many different types of corn. Two types people like to eat are sweet corn and popcorn.

Sweet corn has soft and sweet kernels. When the corn is ripe, the ears are picked from the stalk. The kernels are taken off the cob, and they can be frozen or packed in a can.

Sweet corn can also be eaten from the cob. The ears of corn can be boiled or roasted. This is called eating "corn on the cob."

Popcorn has very hard kernels. They can be yellow, orange, or white. Popcorn kernels are heated until they pop open. The kernels turn inside out and they become light and fluffy. A single ear can make two big bowls of popcorn!

Sometimes people add salt, butter, cheese, or caramel to popcorn. It has been a popular snack for hundreds of years. Long ago, Native Americans and Pilgrims ate it!

Whole kernels are not the only way corn can be eaten. Dried ears of corn can be ground into cornmeal. This can be used to make corn bread, tamales, grits, corn dogs, and cereal. People of all ages enjoy foods made from cornmeal. Many children like to eat corn dogs at the fair.

More Than Food

Corn is not used only as a food. It is sometimes used to make medicine, paper, paints, plastics, and soap. It has even been used to build a palace!

Corn is a plant that we can eat, make things from, and feed to animals. No wonder it is called the bread of life.

Leveled Reading: Social Studies, SV 9781419099656

Name _____ Date _____

 Reading Comprehension Check

Circle the letter next to the **best** answer.

1. Where did corn grow many thousands of years ago?

   A Russia

   B China

   C India

   D Mexico

2. What does the diagram on page 39 show?

   A parts of an ear of corn

   B parts of corn used to make things

   C parts of corn that are left on the stalk

   D parts of an ear of corn that take the longest to grow

3. Which of these foods is made from whole kernels of corn?

   A corn dogs

   B popcorn

   C cereal

   D corn bread

4. Corn husks are important because they—

   A protect the kernels.

   B are food for animals.

   C can be eaten.

   D can be made into baskets.

Answer the questions below in complete sentences.

5. Why does the author tell about three sisters named Corn, Beans, and Squash?

   _____

   _____

6. Why can corn be grown in many places in the world?

   _____

   _____

Name _____ Date _____

 Vocabulary Practice

Write the words from the box to complete the paragraph.

husks	silk	stalks	crop
kernels	maize	cob	legends

Corn was a very important (**1.**) _____ for Native

Americans. They called it (**2.**) _____. It was so important

that they told (**3.**) _____ to explain how corn

first began to grow. Native Americans ate corn, and they used all parts

of the corn plant. For example, they used the (**4.**) _____

when they built their houses.

Corn is also an important food today for people all over the world.

We eat foods made with cornmeal. Cornmeal is made by grinding

dried ears of corn. We also eat whole corn (**5.**) _____,

the small things in rows that look like teeth. These grow on the

(**6.**) _____, which is the core, or inside part, of an ear

of corn. The (**7.**) _____ grow around the ear and protect

the kernels. Corn (**8.**) _____, which is like soft string,

grows inside the husks with the kernels.

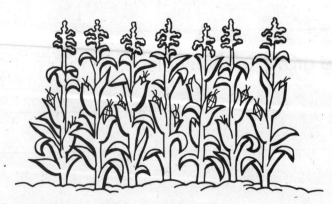

Critical Thinking Activity

1. Make up a menu for a new restaurant. The restaurant is going to serve only foods that are made from corn or that are a type of corn. Use what you have learned from the passage to make the menu. Or look in books or on the Internet to find out about other foods made with corn! Make up a fun name for the restaurant and write it in the box at the top of the menu.

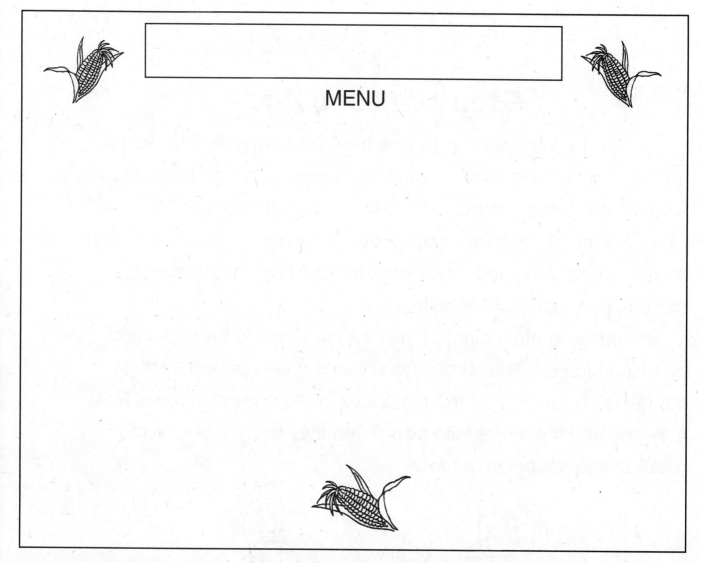

MENU

2. Choose one section of this passage. What is the main idea of this part? What are the details that support the main idea? Use a copy of the Main Idea and Supporting Details Graphic on page 90 to show your answers.

Name _____ Date _____

Think about a popular breakfast: a bowl of cereal with milk. Where did the grains in the cereal come from? Where did the milk come from? You bought the milk and cereal at a store. But before that they came from some kind of farm. Long ago, many people lived on farms. Most of the food they ate came from crops they grew and animals they raised. Find out why they had to work so hard to get food.

Farm Life Long Ago

Long ago, living on a farm was hard work. Families worked together to farm the land. They raised crops to eat and sell. They also raised animals to help with farm work and for food.

Everyone in the family helped out. They got up very early each morning. Everyone had much work to do. They gathered eggs, milked cows, and fed the animals.

In spring, farmers planted their crops. Often farmers planted one kind of seed. They drove horses that pulled **plows** through the fields. Then they placed the seeds in the ground in rows. Next they covered the seeds with **soil.** Then they waited for rain to make the seeds begin to grow.

Most baby animals were born in the spring. Children on the farm often cared for them. They fed the baby animals every day. Children also kept them safe from danger.

In summer, farmers had much work to do. It was often very hot and dry. They had to be sure plants got water. Many farmers built windmills to pull water up from the ground.

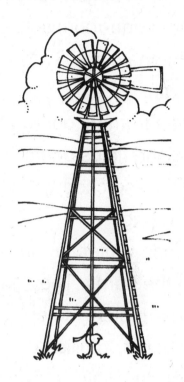

After a hot day of work, farmers rested. They looked for a cool, shady place. Some farmers told stories of days gone by. Children sat near the farmers and listened to the wonderful tales.

Later in summer, some crops were **ripe.** Everyone worked hard to pick them. Horses pulled wagons beside the fields. Farmers put all they had **harvested** into the wagons.

In fall, farmers harvested the last crops. Some crops were canned or dried. Then they were stored for the winter. The rest of the crops were taken to town and sold.

Many towns held a farmers' market. Nearby farmers sold the harvest there. They bought seeds with their money. They also bought clothes and shoes for their families.

Children began school in the fall. They usually went to a one-room school. Children of all ages were in one class. They learned reading, writing, and math.

Then farmers got ready for the winter. They plowed the fields again. They fixed broken fences. Farmers also chopped wood to use for heating and cooking.

During winter, farmers fixed their wagons and plows. They put hay in the barns. They gathered the animals together. Farmers gave them plenty to eat.

In winter, families usually stayed inside. Children learned to cook or build things. Families ate the canned and dried foods they had stored. Hot food kept everyone warm.

Long ago, living on a farm was hard work. Everyone in the family had to help. Today farmers use machines to help. But farming is still very hard work.

Lesson 8: Farm Life Long Ago
Leveled Reading: Social Studies, SV 9781419099656

Name _____ Date _____

 Reading Comprehension Check

Circle the letter next to the **best** answer.

1. According to the passage, which of these did children do on farms?
   A fixed broken fences
   B took care of animals
   C planted crops
   D told stories

2. Farmers fixed their plows *in winter* most likely because—
   A working helped keep them warm.
   B they did not need to use the plows then.
   C fixing the plows was not hard work.
   D they had nothing else to do.

3. Which of these happened in the spring?
   A Crops were sold.
   B Crops were harvested.
   C Crops were canned and stored.
   D Crops were planted.

4. Farming today is different from farming long ago because of—
   A machines.
   B the weather.
   C the kinds of crops.
   D how hard the work is.

Answer the questions below in complete sentences.

5. Why do you think farmers needed to sell their harvest at farmers' markets?

_____

_____

6. Write a summary of what children did on farms long ago.

_____

_____

Lesson 8: Reading Comprehension
Leveled Reading: Social Studies, SV 9781419099656

Name _____ Date _____

 Vocabulary Practice

Circle the letter next to the **best** answer.

1. In this passage, *ripe* means—
   A no longer growing.
   B hard to pick.
   C having a good taste.
   D ready to pick.

2. In this passage, *soil* means—
   A seed.
   B dirt.
   C row.
   D crop.

3. In this passage, *plows* means—
   A tools used for planting.
   B fields where crops are planted.
   C rows where farmers put seeds.
   D wagons pulled by horses.

4. In this passage, *harvested* means—
   A dried.
   B planted.
   C picked.
   D stored.

 Vocabulary Extension

Choose your favorite vocabulary word. Write it in the chart below. Then write what the word means in your own words. Draw a picture to illustrate the word and help you remember it in the future.

Word:	
Definition in my own words:	
Illustration:	

Name _____ Date _____

1. Write two paragraphs. In the first paragraph, tell what you would have liked about living on a farm long ago. In the second paragraph, tell what you would NOT have liked about living on a farm long ago.

_____

_____

_____

_____

_____

_____

_____

_____

_____

_____

_____

2. Think about all the steps in between farmers planting crops and selling them. Use a copy of the Sequence Chain on page 91 to show what a farmer did. Write "Drove a plow through fields" for the first step. Write "Sold the harvest" for the last step.

EXTRA: On a separate sheet of paper, make a chart showing what farmers and their families of long ago did during each season of the year.

Name _____   Date _____

You may have read history books about what life was like for pioneers. But this kind of information is even more interesting when it is in the form of stories. As a young girl, Laura Ingalls Wilder was a pioneer. When she was grown, she wrote interesting books about her life in the 1800s. Read this passage to find out more about this amazing author.

Laura Ingalls Wilder: An Author's Story

On February 7, 1867, Laura Ingalls was born in the big woods of Wisconsin. Life there was hard. The winters were long and cold.

The Ingalls family lived in a small log cabin built by Laura's father, Charles. He farmed and hunted for food to feed his family. Laura called him Pa. Her mother took care of the house and the children.

Laura's family moved many times. Pa always wanted to move west to **settle.** When Laura was two, they moved to the flat **prairie** of Kansas.

The Ingalls family traveled in a covered wagon pulled by horses. At night, they camped by the wagon. They made a fire to keep warm and to cook with. They slept under the stars. When it rained, the family **huddled** in the wagon. It was hard to move the whole family in a covered wagon.

The Kansas prairie land was very different from Wisconsin. It was flat and dry. Tall grasses blew back and forth in the winds. There were no hills and few trees. The winters were long, and there were many storms. It was harder to farm on the prairie than in Wisconsin.

In Kansas, the Ingalls family lived in another log house built by Pa. At night, Pa played the **fiddle.** Everyone laughed and sang. In time, they began to get used to Kansas life. Then Laura's father learned that they could have their Wisconsin land back. So the family moved back to the big woods.

They stayed only one year in Wisconsin. When Laura was seven, Pa moved the family to Minnesota and started a farm. There they lived in a little dugout house. It was built on the side of a hill by a creek. It had one door and one window. The roof was made of sod, or grass.

Laura and her sisters went to a one-room school in town. Pa grew tall fields of wheat. One day, many thousands of grasshoppers came through and ate all their crops. They could not save the farm. So the family had to move again. This time, they moved to nearby Iowa.

Name _____ Date _____

Laura was happy in Iowa. Pa worked at a hotel in Iowa. But he missed the wide open spaces of the country. Soon the Ingalls family moved back to Minnesota again.

There Laura's sister Mary got very sick. Mary had a **fever** and almost died. She became blind. Pa asked Laura to promise to be Mary's eyes for her. After that, Laura always told Mary everything she saw.

Then Pa heard he could get a job working on the railroads. Soon the family moved again. This time, they traveled to South Dakota.

Life in South Dakota was very hard. Summers were hot, and the winters were freezing cold. One winter, a **blizzard** hit the town. Store owners had kept only a little food for sale in the stores. Soon that ran out. But the blizzard went on. Snow was so deep that people could not get out of their houses. No trains could get into town with food. People almost **starved** to death that long winter.

At last, a strong young man from Laura's town made it through the blizzard to another town. He brought back food for many people. His name was Almanzo Wilder. Laura liked this brave young man.

When Laura was only 15, she began teaching school. At first, students made her **nervous.** But then she took control. The job was not close to home. Each weekend, Almanzo gave her a ride home.

Laura married Almanzo Wilder when she was 18. In 1886, they had a daughter named Rose. She was named after the prairie flowers her mother loved. Almanzo wanted to be a farmer, but these were hard years for them. Their crops died. Almanzo became sick and almost died.

After a few years, the Wilder family moved to Missouri. Winters were **mild** there. They bought a farm with a little log house. Laura loved the apple trees on the farm. At last, she was settled in one place.

The Wilders worked hard on their farm. It was during these years that Laura told Rose stories of her early life on the prairie. She told what it was like to travel in a covered wagon. She told what it was like to live in a dugout house. She told what it was like when a blizzard hit.

Rose grew up and became an author. She always remembered her mother's stories. Rose asked Laura to write these stories down. At the age of 65, Laura Ingalls Wilder became an author.

She wrote her first children's book in between doing farm chores. It took her over a year to do this. But the time and work were worth it. Her first book, named *Little House in the Big Woods,* became a big hit.

Name _____ Date _____

✓ Reading Comprehension Check

Answer each question in complete sentences.

1. From what the author says about Pa, what can you tell about him?

_____

_____

2. When Pa asked Laura to "promise to be Mary's eyes for her," what did he mean?

_____

_____

3. Why do you think Laura married Almanzo Wilder?

_____

_____

4. Near the end, the author says, "At last, she was settled in one place." What does this tell you about Laura Ingalls Wilder?

_____

_____

5. Why did Laura Ingalls Wilder become an author?

_____

_____

6. How do you know this passage is a biography?

_____

_____

Name _____ Date _____

 Vocabulary Practice

Write the words from the box to complete the paragraph.

starved	huddled	prairie
mild	blizzard	nervous
settle	fever	fiddle

When the Ingalls family moved from Wisconsin to Kansas, many

pioneers were going west. They wanted to (**1.**) _____ in

places where fewer people lived. The trip was never safe or easy.

Many families crossed the flat (**2.**) _____ and traveled

into mountains. If the families were traveling in winter, they might be

caught in a (**3.**) _____. While they waited for the storm to

pass, they (**4.**) _____ in their wagons to stay warm. If a

child got sick from the bad weather and had a (**5.**) _____,

there was no doctor around. Mothers and fathers would be very (**6.**)

_____ until their child was well again. Sometimes families

ran out of food during the bad weather. If they could not hunt for food or

get food from other families, they sometimes (**7.**) _____.

Yet the trip west was not all bad. When the weather was

(**8.**) _____, people would gather around a campfire. They

would tell stories. Sometimes a person would play the

(**9.**) _____ and everyone would sing until it was time to go

to sleep.

Leveled Reading: Social Studies, SV 9781419099656

Critical Thinking Activity

I. In your own words, describe Laura Ingalls Wilder's life.

_____

_____

_____

_____

_____

_____

_____

_____

_____

_____

_____

_____

_____

2. Compare and contrast the Ingalls family's life in Kansas with their life in Wisconsin the first time they lived there. Use a copy of the Compare and Contrast Chart on page 92 to show your answers. In the Topics box, write "Life in Wisconsin and Life in Kansas."

Name _____ Date _____

Think about a large city you have lived in, read about, or visited. There are most likely lots of cars and buses, large buildings, and big crowds of people in that city. But what makes it different from other large cities? What makes it special? In this passage, you will read about four large cities in very different parts of the world. How do these cities compare with the city you are thinking about?

Cities Around the World

There are many beautiful cities around the world. Each one is special in its own way. All cities have many people, interesting places to see, and lots of things to do.

The four cities you will read about are all very different from each other. In the first city, people celebrate when cherry trees blossom. In the second one, people to go the square where their president lives in a palace. In the third city, people ice skate in a park. In the fourth one, people go to museums to see things that are thousands of years old.

Washington, D.C.

Washington, D.C., is the **capital** of the United States. A capital is the city where many of a country's leaders work. They make the laws of the country there. Washington, D.C., is named after the first president of the United States, George Washington.

Washington, D.C., has many museums, parks, and zoos. The National Zoo has many kinds of animals. It even has some pandas and gorillas. Each year thousands of people visit the amazing zoo.

The most famous house in the United States is the White House. This is where the president of the United States lives. Many people visit the White House each year.

Washington, D.C., has many other famous buildings and **monuments.** The tallest one is the Washington Monument. People take the elevator to the top of the monument to see great views of the city.

Washington, D.C., also has monuments named for President Lincoln and for President Jefferson. These buildings are on park land. Speeches, concerts, and parades are held there on holidays.

Many people visit Washington, D.C., in the month of April for cherry blossom time. Years ago the people of Japan gave the United States many cherry trees as a gift. The cherry trees are planted all around the city. When the cherry trees bloom, there is a large festival to celebrate. People eat Japanese food, listen to music, and watch a parade. Everyone enjoys the beautiful cherry blossoms.

Mexico City

Mexico City is a very large city in the center of Mexico. It is the capital of the country. It is one of the largest cities in the world. It has a **subway** to help move all the many people around the city underground.

Mexico City is in a low area that has mountains all around it. The weather in Mexico City is mild and warm, even in the winter. During the summer, it rains almost every day.

In downtown Mexico City, there is a large square. On one side of the square is the palace where the president of Mexico lives. Offices and Mexico's largest church are on the other three sides of the square. The middle of the square is a public meeting place, and it looks like a small park. People can decorate the square for special events, such as the Independence Day Fiesta. Then people wear special clothes and sing and dance. Streets are closed off to cars so people can walk and dance in the streets.

Mexico City has museums, parks, churches, and a zoo. In an art museum, you might see paintings by the famous Mexican artist Diego Rivera. Or you might see paintings of dancers with colorful clothes.

A favorite place to visit in Mexico City is the market. People sell handmade pottery, jewelry, baskets, and much more there. The people are proud of their work and enjoy showing it to those people who visit the market.

What do people do for fun in Mexico City? Sometimes they go to soccer games or baseball games. These are the most popular sports in Mexico. Many families go together to see their favorite players.

Most of the people in Mexico do not work on Sundays. On that day they relax in a park or at home. They might enjoy a picnic together or visit their families.

Moscow

Moscow is the largest city in Russia. It is also the capital city. It is usually cool or cold there. Moscow is on a large river, so it is a **port** city. This means that ships bring in **supplies** and then take Moscow's goods to other places.

Moscow is a very old city, but it is becoming modern. The city is growing and changing. New stores and hotels are being built next to old palaces and churches.

Name _____ Date _____

Moscow was built in the shape of a wheel. Two main roads circle the city. Other roads are like spokes that come from the middle of the wheel.

In the center of Moscow is the Kremlin. It is an old **fort.** It has a wall around it in the shape of a triangle. There are twenty towers on the wall. Inside the wall are old palaces and churches. It is like a city inside a city.

Red Square is a large open area next to the Kremlin. Here there are many stores, hotels, museums, and beautiful old churches. Just as in Mexico City, special days are celebrated in the square. People watch parades, and the bells in the churches ring.

To have fun, many people in Moscow go to Gorki Park. This huge park has many rides. There is also a lake with paddle boats and canoes. People ice-skate on the lake in winter.

In Moscow, **ballet** dancing is very popular. There is a famous ballet school in Moscow. Many of the students of this school have become superstars and toured the world.

Cairo

Cairo is the capital of Egypt. It is also the largest city in all of Africa. Like the city of Moscow, it is a busy port city. Ships sail down the Nile River to carry goods in and out of Cairo.

Cairo is a crowded city. People hurry to work and to shop. Streets are full of cars and buses. Sidewalk markets line the streets.

In the center of Cairo is a square. It is a big, open area with grass and sidewalks where people can meet. Many tall, new buildings are all around the square. Some are stores, hotels, and office buildings.

Cairo is growing. Many people move to Cairo each week. To help people travel, the first subway in Africa was built in Cairo in 1987. Today many people use the subway.

Many years ago, the rulers of Egypt built monuments called the **pyramids.** The pyramids were made of many blocks of stone. Thousands of years ago, the rulers of Egypt were buried with their treasures in the pyramids.

Many treasures from the pyramids are in a Cairo museum. There you can also see the **mummies** of the ancient rulers and their gold jewelry. It is almost like stepping back in time.

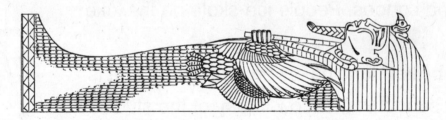

You have read about four different cities around the world. They are all different from each other, but some things are the same. Each of the cities is a capital. Each city has a central square for festivals. Each city has parks, museums, and other places to have fun. You can learn more about these cities in the library. You can also learn about many other beautiful and interesting cities around the world. Someday you might even visit them!

Name _____ Date _____

 Reading Comprehension Check

Circle the letter next to the **best** answer.

1. The author says you can go to a zoo in—
   A the capitals of Russia and Egypt.
   B the capitals of Russia and the United States.
   C the capitals of Egypt and Mexico.
   D the capitals of Mexico and the United States.

2. Which of the four cities is the largest?
   A Mexico City
   B Washington, D.C.
   C Moscow
   D Cairo

3. How is Cairo different from Moscow?
   A Only Cairo is growing.
   B There are things thousands of years old only in Cairo.
   C Only Cairo is a port city.
   D There is a large square only in Cairo.

4. In which city do you know for sure that it is cool or cold most of the time?
   A Washington, D.C.
   B Mexico City
   C Moscow
   D Cairo

5. What do Mexico City and Moscow have in common?
   A ice-skating on lakes
   B celebrations in a square
   C the weather
   D the shape of the city

6. What is the BEST caption for the picture on page 58?
   A People can see the Kremlin from this building.
   B This is the National Zoo.
   C A very important person lives in this building.
   D Many monuments like this one are in Washington, D.C.

Name _____ Date _____

 Vocabulary Practice

Choose a word from the box to complete each sentence. Write each word on the line.

capital	subway	ballet	Monuments	supplies
Pyramids	fort	port	Mummies	

1. A _____ is a city next to water where ships can land.

2. A _____ is a train that runs underground.

3. A _____ is a kind of dance that tells a story.

4. In a country's _____, the leaders make laws.

5. _____ are buildings made to remember a person or event.

6. A _____ is a strong building where people are protected.

7. _____ are the bodies of kings, queens, and other rulers from long ago.

8. _____ are huge stone monuments built by people long ago.

9. Steel and wood are kinds of _____, which are used to make goods.

 Vocabulary Extension

Write a word in each box that will help you remember what the word in each oval means.

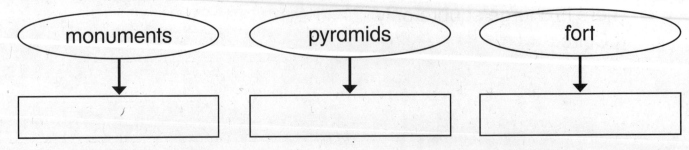

monuments   pyramids   fort

Name _____   Date _____

 Critical Thinking Activity

1. Draw something in each box that is a symbol for the city. Write a label under each symbol.

Moscow	Cairo
_____	_____

Mexico City	Washington, D.C.
_____	_____

2. Which of these four cities would you like to visit the most? Tell why.

_____

_____

_____

Name _____   Date _____

Exploring a place for the first time can be an adventure. The place may be a city. It may be a forest. Exploring is even more of an adventure if you don't have a map or any information about the place. Can you imagine what it was like to be an explorer of a new land long ago—without any maps and with little information about the place? Read this passage to learn about explorers.

Explorers: Searching for Adventure

Explorers travel to **faraway** places and return home to tell about their journeys. Some explorers start their new adventures on land. Some have underwater adventures. Explorers even go into outer space.

For thousands of years, people have wanted to learn about all the different places on Earth. Some explored to find better places to live, while other explorers searched for food or drinking water. Some looked for treasure and adventure.

First explorers found the seven continents on Earth. A globe shows the continents as large chunks of land. Great oceans and seas cover the rest of Earth.

Over hundreds of years, people explored some continents by walking. Other continents could be reached only by ships. People explored the continents around the North Pole and the South Pole by using dog sleds across the snow and ice.

The first explorers traveled by land and by water. There were many tools to help them. Wheels made travel over land easier. Carts and wagons made it easier for people to carry food, clothes, and supplies. Rafts, boats, and sails let people travel over water.

Travelers used maps and charts to find good **routes** to places. They used compasses to help them go in the right direction. They also used the sun and the stars to find their way.

Early Explorers

The Vikings were people who lived in northern Europe about 1,000 years ago. They traveled over land and over water in search of new farmland. The Vikings were some of the first people to explore new places by ship.

One Viking explorer, Eric the Red, sailed to a new land that he named Greenland. Later, his son, Leif Ericson, traveled even farther south to a land where grapes were growing. So he named that land Wineland. He left no maps, so no one is sure where that land was.

Many years later, 2 brothers from Italy went on a long trip to Asia. They were Maffeo and Nicolo Polo. The trip took 9 years. Later Nicolo's son, Marco Polo, traveled with them to Asia. He was only 17 years old when he left home.

Marco Polo returned home from the big adventure 24 years later! He had traveled nearly 15,000 miles. He wrote a book about all his exciting adventures. The book made others want to explore new places, too.

About 200 years later, Prince Henry of Portugal did something to help explorers. He opened a school to teach sailors how to find their way on the open water. This study of finding good routes for travel is called navigation.

Prince Henry wanted sailors to explore the **oceans.** He paid for many of their **voyages.** After that time, most of Earth could be explored and mapped.

Around the World

Christopher Columbus was an Italian mapmaker. He believed the world was round, not flat. Not many people agreed with him. He believed that he could travel to Asia by sailing across the Atlantic Ocean.

It took Columbus 7 years to get enough money to pay for the trip. Finally King Ferdinand and Queen Isabella of Spain helped him with ships and money. With 3 ships and a crew of 120 men, he set sail for Asia.

Leveled Reading: Social Studies, SV 9781419099656

But the three ships landed on an island. Columbus had landed in a different place than he expected. He had landed in what is now called the Americas. Columbus later made three more voyages to the Americas, but he never reached Asia.

Many great explorers followed the route of Columbus. Stories of his trips led more people to explore North America and South America.

After the travels of Christopher Columbus, Ferdinand Magellan also thought he could find a route to Asia by sea. In 1519, he set sail with 5 ships and 241 crew members. On the way, they had bad weather, illness, and shipwrecks. Magellan and many other men died on the trip.

After 3 long years, only 1 ship with 18 men left on it got back home. They had **proved** that it was possible to sail all the way around Earth. One man wrote down the events of the voyage so many people learned about sailing the oceans.

Exploring the Americas

As more people settled in the Americas, explorers drew maps and wrote about the mountains, deserts, and rivers. They wrote about plants and animals and the people they met on their travels.

In the early 1800s, Meriwether Lewis and William Clark explored and mapped much of the United States. With the help of Sacagawea, a Native American, Lewis and Clark traveled up the Missouri River. They crossed over the Rocky Mountains and went on west to the Pacific Ocean. Then they traveled all the way back east to Missouri. They had explored 6,000 miles of new land in 2 years!

Name _____ Date _____

To the Poles

Until the early 1900s, the North Pole and the South Pole
had not been explored. Both are covered with ice and snow
all year long. Robert Peary and Matthew Henson
had tried many times to reach the North Pole.
Peary sailed a ship that moved through ice. They
traveled over ice fields on land with dog sleds.
They finally reached the North Pole in 1909.

Matthew Henson

Later 2 groups of explorers raced to reach
the South Pole. Roald Amundsen's great skill
with dog sleds helped his group get to the South
Pole 5 weeks before another group arrived in 1911.

Deep Seas and High Mountains

Life under the seas had not been explored. Jacques Cousteau
was one of the first to explore life under the sea. He invented
special tools to help explore the oceans. He helped invent gear
for divers so they could breathe underwater.

Beginning in 1951, Cousteau led a special research ship.
The crew made maps of the ocean floor and studied sea life.
They measured water flow and temperature. They also searched
for oil and minerals. Cousteau wrote books and made **films**
about sea life.

Leveled Reading: Social Studies, SV 9781419099656

Not only did people explore the deepest seas, but they also explored the highest mountains. The highest mountain on Earth is Mount Everest.

Many mountain climbers had tried to climb this steep mountain, where there are high winds and thin air. Then in 1953, Sir Edmund Hillary and his guide, Tenzing Norgay, reached the top. It was a brave adventure. Since then other climbers have reached the top of Mount Everest and have studied many mountains.

Into Space

Explorers have studied many places on Earth, and some explorers have even been to outer space. In 1961, a Russian pilot named Yuri Gagarin was the first to travel in space to orbit Earth.

In 1969, Neil Armstrong and Edwin Aldrin were the first people to walk on the moon. In 1996, Dr. Shannon Lucid spent 188 days studying Earth aboard a Russian space station. That is a long time to be away from Earth!

There are many places to be explored. New explorers might learn more about mountains, caves, deserts, oceans, and outer space. They might learn more about rocks from the moon or from other planets. Who knows what might be **discovered** next? Maybe you will be the next explorer to find out.

Name _____   Date _____

✓ Reading Comprehension Check

Complete each sentence below.

1. Other people became interested in exploring new, unknown places after Marco Polo _____

_____.

2. _____ was not an explorer, but he

helped explorers by _____

_____.

3. Some explorers did things that helped later explorers. One example

is _____ ,

who _____.

4. Something that was a great disappointment to Christopher Columbus

was that _____

_____.

5. The main idea of the part of the passage called "Exploring the

Americas" is that _____

_____

_____

6. One thing that Meriwether Lewis and William Clark had in common

with Jacques Cousteau was that _____

_____.

Leveled Reading: Social Studies, SV 9781419099656

Name _____ Date _____

 Vocabulary Practice

Choose a word from the box that can take the place of the underlined word in the sentence. Write the word on the line.

faraway	voyages	films	discovered
oceans	route	proved	

1. Some explorers followed the same <u>path</u> that earlier explorers had

   followed. _____

2. Columbus made four <u>trips</u> to the Americas. _____

3. In the 1900s, people explored mountains, <u>seas</u>, and outer space.

   _____

4. Magellan's travels <u>showed</u> that people could travel by ship all the way

   around Earth. _____

5. Explorers traveled to <u>distant</u> lands. _____

6. Cousteau made <u>movies</u> so that others could learn about sea life.

   _____

7. Some explorers <u>found</u> lands they had not expected to be there.

   _____

 Vocabulary Extension

Choose two vocabulary words. Describe something that is an example and something that is not an example for each word.

Word:	Word:
Example:	Example:
Non-example:	Non-example:

Name _____ Date _____

Critical Thinking Activity

1. Read the last paragraph of the passage again. If you were an explorer, which of the things named in the paragraph would you like to learn more about? Explain your answer.

_____

_____

_____

_____

_____

_____

_____

_____

_____

_____

2. Make a time line showing people who explored land, sea, and outer space between the early 1800s and 1996. There are eight of these explorers (or pairs of explorers) and their important dates named in the passage. Use a copy of the Time Line on page 93 to show your answers. Be sure to give your time line a title.

EXTRA: Name important inventions used by some of the people you showed in your time line. Write the years the things were invented. Find out this information in books or on the Internet.

Name _____ Date _____

Have you ever wanted to do something but people or events got in
your way of doing it? Did you finally do what you wanted to do?
Charles Bolden, a pilot of the space shuttle *Columbia,* did just that.
Read about the people and events that got in his way and the
amazing things he did.

The Perseverance of Charles F. Bolden, Jr.

Charles F. Bolden, Jr., worked very hard as a high school
student in South Carolina. His high grades made him a member
of the National Honor Society. He served as editor of the school
newspaper and president of the student council. He was also a
member of the chorus and the athletic club. He **persevered** in his
studies and graduated second in his class in 1964.

Still, Charles had to overcome **obstacles** when he tried to get
into college. The University of South Carolina turned him down.
No African American had ever attended that university. Charles's
mother and father found out about schools outside South Carolina.
Going away to college in another state would cost more, but his
parents were **determined** that he should go. Charles wanted to go
to college more than anything.

After reading about the United States Naval Academy, Charles
said to his dad, "I really want to join the Marine Corps. The Academy
is where I should go." But his father knew that Charles would need
a sponsor from South Carolina to write a letter supporting Charles.
At that time African Americans had a hard time finding support.

Name _____ Date _____

Charles tried anyway. He wrote to South Carolina's members of Congress. He even wrote to the vice president of the United States, Lyndon Johnson. He received a letter of support from Vice President Johnson. But Charles had to have the support of someone in Congress. In spite of Charles's efforts, no one from South Carolina wrote a letter.

Charles was disappointed. But he did not give up. He knew that somehow there had to be a way. He continued to write to anyone who might help. He was determined to overcome this **challenge.** When Vice President Johnson became president of the United States in 1963, Charles wrote to him again.

Charles's **persistence** paid off. In 1964, he heard that William L. Dawson, an African American congressman from Chicago, had agreed to sponsor him for the Naval Academy. After many letters and much hard work, Charles entered the Naval Academy in 1964.

Like all students at the Naval Academy, Charles found the classes difficult. He had to learn other languages, study math and different sciences, and still go through very tough war training.

At that time, few African Americans had studied at the Academy. It was hard being one of the few African Americans among thousands of students at the academy. But Charles was ready for the challenge. He made friends with his classmates, and he impressed his teachers. Charles became the first African American class president in the history of the Naval Academy. He graduated from the Academy in 1968.

When Charles graduated, he married his high-school sweetheart, Alexis "Jackie" Walker of Columbia. Their son, Anthony Ché, was born on June 9, 1971. Their daughter, Kelly, was born on March 17, 1976.

The next step in Charles's plan was to join the Marine Corps. Only a small number of Naval Academy graduates could move on to the Marine Corps, but Charles was selected. He went through the difficult six-month training period, where he learned the basic skills of being a soldier. He graduated second in his basic-training class. Charles then decided he wanted to become a marine pilot.

For the next two years, Charles learned how to fly planes. He trained in Florida, Mississippi, and Texas. Soon he was fighting in the Vietnam War. He piloted more than 100 flights during the war. Sometimes Charles and his crew flew at night. Sometimes they flew in bad weather. During the entire year Charles served in the war, he was always able to guide his plane safely back to base.

During that time, Charles was also training to become a test pilot for the Navy. In 1979, he made an important decision. He decided to apply to become an astronaut. In 1980, he was chosen as an astronaut **candidate.** There were 78 astronauts at that time. Only 4 were African Americans.

Name _____ Date _____

Charles's astronaut training lasted a year. He learned how to make emergency repairs and how to walk in space. He also learned how to fly a space shuttle. Then he waited for five years. Finally in 1986, Charles flew on his first flight into space as the pilot of the space shuttle *Columbia.*

General Bolden has traveled around the United States to visit schools and talk to students. He reminds them of how important it is to stay in school. "Mainly," he says, "have a dream. Don't sell yourself short. Believe you can do it, and you will."

Ethel Bolden, Charles's mother, still lives in the home where Charles grew up. She is proud of her son. She says that Charles faced many challenges on the road to becoming an astronaut. He had to study and work hard to make good grades in school. She says that his strongest talent is that he knew how hard the work would be and he did it anyway.

General Bolden has received many honors and awards for his hard work and special abilities. One very special award was an honorary Doctor of Science Degree from the University of South Carolina in 1984. This is the same college that turned him away 20 years earlier. Another award came in February 13, 1999, when General Bolden was made a member of the South Carolina Hall of Fame.

Charles said of his first flight into space, "It was more than I had ever dreamed of—a fantastic, **uplifting** experience. I can't explain all the feelings, but I know for sure there's something out there other than space." And after flying four more voyages into space, he still feels the same way.

The city of Columbia, South Carolina, and the rest of the United States are very proud of their native son, who overcame many challenges in order to make his dreams come true. To people everywhere, he says, "You can, too."

✓ Reading Comprehension Check

Answer each question in complete sentences.

1. Why did Charles have to go to college in another state?

_____

_____

2. Why was studying at the United States Naval Academy harder for Charles than for most of the other students?

_____

_____

3. Read the paragraph on page 76 again that begins with "Charles tried anyway." Do you think that South Carolina's members of Congress changed how they thought about him after Charles flew the space shuttle? Explain your answer.

_____

_____

4. What is a detail in the passage that shows that Charles was determined to get into the Naval Academy?

_____

_____

5. What tells you that this passage is a biography?

_____

_____

6. Why did the author most likely write this passage?

_____

_____

Name _____ Date _____

 Vocabulary Practice

Choose a word from the box to complete each sentence. Write each word on the line.

obstacles	uplifting	persistence	challenge
determined	candidate	persevered	

1. A boy who shows _____ keeps trying even though he has failed at something.

2. A _____ is a person who wants and prepares for a job.

3. The opposite of *gave up* is _____.

4. People or things that stand in the way of someone's goals are

   _____.

5. A girl who accepts a _____ is ready to make an effort to overcome something difficult.

6. Athletes who are _____ do not stop practicing after they lose a race or a game.

7. A compound word that means "making a person feel better about

   himself or herself" is _____.

 Vocabulary Extension

Choose your favorite vocabulary word. Complete the graphic organizer.

Word:	
Looks like:	
Sounds like:	
Feels like:	
Synonym:	

Leveled Reading: Social Studies, SV 9781419099656

Name _____ Date _____

🔆 Critical Thinking Activity

I. Write a paragraph to describe a challenge you have overcome. Explain what the challenge is and everything you have done to overcome it. Include many details in your paragraph.

_____

_____

_____

_____

_____

_____

_____

_____

_____

_____

_____

_____

2. Think of a famous person you have read about who has overcome a challenge. How is this person like Charles Bolden, Jr.? How is this person different? Use a copy of the the Compare and Contrast Chart on page 92 to show your answers.

Name _____   Date _____

The president of the United States is a very important person with a very important job. Do you know why? Do you know what the president's duties are? Read this passage to find out. You'll be surprised when you discover how much the president has to do!

The U.S. President

When the Constitution of the United States was written, the writers did not list every one of the president's duties. They depended on George Washington to work out many of the president's responsibilities. They knew he would set a good example for the presidents to come. Today the president has many duties that keep him or her very, very busy.

Chief Executive

Because the president is the **head** of the Executive Branch of the U.S. government, he or she is often called the Chief Executive. In this role he or she must make sure that all of the country's laws and **treaties** are carried out. The president must decide how much money the country should spend and prepare a **budget.** He or she must also direct all groups of people that carry out the business of the country.

The members of the president's Cabinet are part of the Executive Branch. Cabinet members advise the president. All are heads of important departments of government, such as education, health, and energy.

As Chief Executive, the president has emergency powers. These powers allow him or her to end or prevent emergencies that threaten national safety or health. The president can also give executive orders. These orders are statements or directions that have the force of laws. President Lincoln gave an executive order in 1863 when he declared that all slaves were free.

Commander in Chief

The president is also the leader of the U.S. **military.** His or her job is to make sure the country is safe in times of peace and that it is protected in times of war. As commander in chief, the president is in charge of the army, navy, air force, and marines. He or she can send troops overseas. However, the president cannot declare war on another country.

Head of State

Another of the president's jobs is to represent the government of the United States. The president attends special celebrations such as the opening of a national park. He or she travels all over the United States and to many **foreign** countries. He or she invites leaders of other countries to the United States and the White House. He or she also gives awards to war heroes and invites important people from the United States to the White House.

Director of Foreign Affairs

One of the most difficult jobs of the president is to direct the country's relationships with foreign countries. The president **appoints** people to travel to other countries and represent the United States. The president has the power to make treaties with other countries to end wars or disagreements. He or she can refuse to speak with new foreign governments. He or she can also suggest laws that help them. Some presidents have acted as world peacemakers. They have helped other countries to work out problems. For example, Woodrow Wilson helped work out the peace treaty that ended World War I.

Lawmaking Leader

The president cannot **pass** new laws. Only the U.S. Congress can do that. However, one of the president's jobs is to suggest new laws. These proposed laws are called **bills.** Each year the president gives a speech to Congress called the State of the Union Address. In this speech, the president describes bills that he or she would like Congress to turn into laws.

The Leader of the People

Perhaps the most important of all the president's jobs is to serve all U.S. citizens, not just one state or one person. To lead and inform the people, he or she must communicate with them. Early presidents made speeches to groups of people. Later presidents used radio. Franklin Roosevelt used radio programs he called "fireside chats." Roosevelt also used TV to speak to the people. He was the first president to do this. Since the 1960s, presidents have mainly used TV to communicate with the U.S. public.

Electing the President

Many people would like to be president, but not everyone can be. The Constitution has rules about who can be president. The person must be at least 35 years old. He or she must have been born in the United States. In addition, he or she must have lived in the United States for 14 years or longer.

Election Day is the first Tuesday in November every four years. On that day, people vote for the person they think will make the best president.

The president serves the United States for four years. This is called his or her term of office. Then there is another election. The president can be elected again for a second term.

The president is powerful, but the voters have even more power. If they do not like a president, they do not have to elect that person for a second term. "The president *is* commander in chief," Franklin Roosevelt told future presidents, "[but] he, too, has superior officers—the people of the United States."

Name _____ Date _____

Circle the letter next to the **best** answer.

1. Which of these was an executive order given by the president in 1863?

   A sending troops to another country

   B suggesting a law to be passed by Congress

   C freeing people who were slaves

   D working out a peace treaty to end a war

2. Which of these can a U.S. president NOT do?

   A refuse to speak to other presidents

   B declare war on another country

   C use emergency powers after a hurricane

   D represent the U.S. government

3. Which president helped countries who were at war?

   A Abraham Lincoln

   B Franklin Roosevelt

   C Woodrow Wilson

   D George Washington

4. Which of these is an opinion?

   A "They knew he would set a good example for the presidents to come."

   B "His or her job is to make sure the country is safe in times of peace."

   C "However, one of the president's jobs is to suggest new laws."

   D "Perhaps the most important of all the president's jobs is to serve all U.S. citizens."

Answer the question below in complete sentences.

5. Use your own words to name a detail that supports this main idea from the passage: "Another of the president's jobs is to represent the government of the United States."

_____

_____

Name _____ Date _____

 Vocabulary Practice

Circle the letter next to the **best** answer.

1. In this passage, *foreign* means—
   A having to do with another country.
   B a country wanting to trade goods and ideas.
   C a country where fewer people live.
   D a more powerful country.

2. In this passage, *military* means—
   A all the heroes from a war.
   B groups that start wars.
   C all of a country's army, navy, air force, and marine troops.
   D money used to pay for a war.

3. In this passage, *bills* means—
   A things that have to be paid.
   B the front part of caps.
   C possible new laws.
   D paper money.

4. In this passage, *appoints* means—
   A persuades someone to do a job.
   B orders a person to do a job.
   C expects someone to do a job.
   D chooses a person to do a job.

5. In this passage, *budget* means a plan for—
   A how groups will be directed.
   B how laws will be carried out.
   C how money will be spent.
   D how business will be done.

6. In this passage, *pass* means—
   A to vote for.
   B to go ahead of someone.
   C to not have a turn.
   D to come to an end.

7. In this passage, *treaties* means—
   A the laws of another country.
   B formal agreements made between countries.
   C orders given by the president.
   D speeches made to inform people.

8. In this passage, *head* means—
   A the top part of something.
   B a subject or topic.
   C most important.
   D a person in charge of something.

Name _____ Date _____

1. What is the main idea of the section called "Director of Foreign Affairs"? What are the details that support the main idea? Use a copy of the Main Idea and Supporting Details Graphic on page 90 to show your answers.

2. The author describes the following kinds of duties of a U.S. president: Chief Executive, Commander in Chief, Head of State, Director of Foreign Affairs, and Lawmaking Leader. In your opinion, which of these kinds of duties is the most important? Tell why you think this.

_____

_____

_____

_____

_____

_____

_____

_____

_____

_____

_____

EXTRA: Read about a U.S. president. On a separate sheet of paper, write about some important things he or she did. Tell what kind of duty each thing was.

Main Idea and Supporting Details Graphic

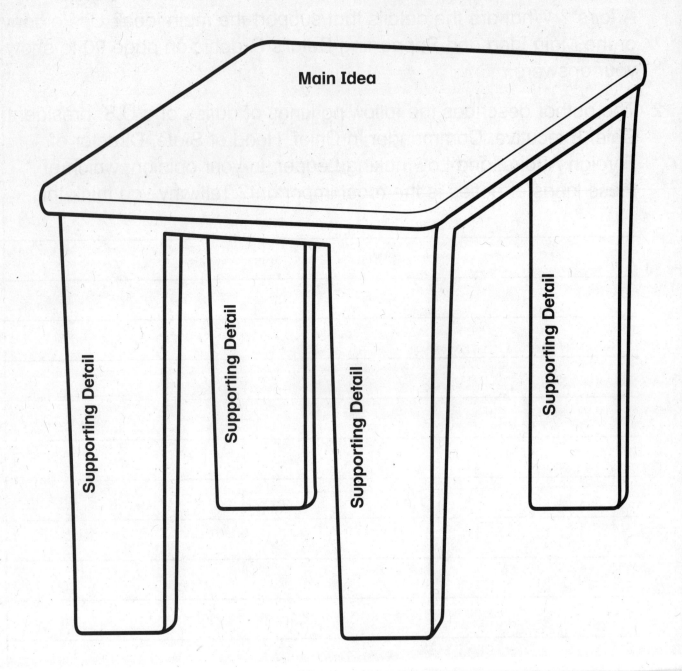

Name _____ Date _____

Sequence Chain

Title _____

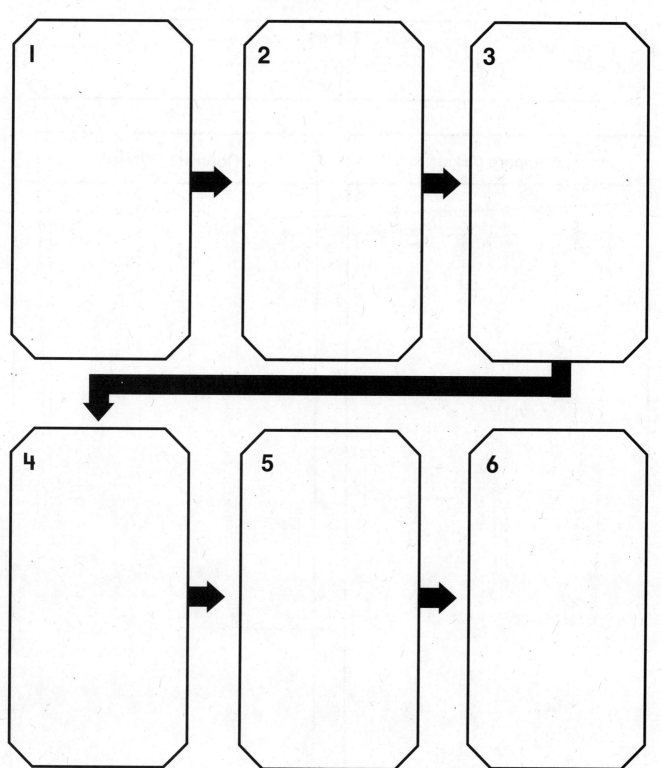

1

2

3

4

5

6

Sequence Chain
Leveled Reading: Social Studies, SV 9781419099656

Name _____ Date _____

Compare and Contrast Chart

Title _____

Topics

Compare (Alike)	**Contrast** (Different)

Compare and Contrast Chart
Leveled Reading: Social Studies, SV 9781419099656

Name _____ Date _____

Time Line

Title _____

Leveled Reading: Social Studies, SV 9781419099656

Time Line

Page 7
1. there is a lot to do
2. the bakery and the supermarket
3. a post office
4. the park
5. go to the library
6. go to the bakery or the supermarket
7. the park
8. Sample answer: a neighborhood is a busy place

Page 8
1. B
2. A
3. C
4. D
Pictures will vary.

Page 9
1. Map will vary. Places should be labeled.
2. Answers will vary.
3. Answers will vary.

Page 11
1. B
2. A
3. D
4. D
5. C
6. A
7. Roberta Bondar was the first Canadian woman in outer space.

Page 12
Across
1. satellites
3. telescope
6. orbit
7. scientists
Down
2. astronauts
4. distant
5. photos

Page 13
Diary entries will vary but should include details from the passage.

Page 16
1. B
2. D
3. C
4. A
5. Sample answer: At both Mardi Gras and the new year festival in Vietnam, people watch parades and eat a special food.
6. People are most likely celebrating the lemon harvest.

Page 17
1. pudding
2. fritters
3. tortillas
4. icing
5. festivals
6. floats
Answers will vary.

Page 18
Answers will vary.

Page 21
1. Blubber helps seals and walruses stay warm when it is very cold.
2. Arctic winters are harsh, and in some places the sun never rises. Snow covers the land, and ice covers the ocean. In the summer it stays snowy in some places, but in other places it gets warm and the sun never sets.
3. Both the Inuit and Lapps live in the Arctic. For both groups, some people live in a modern way, while others move around a lot to hunt for food or follow animal herds.
4. Arctic hares have white fur so they cannot be seen easily against the white snow.

5. The author most likely wrote this passage to tell readers about the weather, animals, and people of the Arctic.
6. Sample answer: Even though the Arctic may be a very cold place, there is plenty of life there.

Page 22
1. melts
2. herds
3. igloos
4. modern
5. blubber
6. harsh
7. layer
Vocabulary word examples will vary.

Page 23
Part 1
1. Arctic foxes and hares stay warm.
2. layer of fat (blubber)
3. Reindeer can walk on snow.
4. to be with their reindeer, which are looking for food
5. The sun never rises.
Part 2
Answers will vary.

Page 27
1. B
2. A
3. A
4. D
5. B
6. C

Page 28
Across
3. courtyards
5. towers
6. enemies
7. feasts
Down
1. moats
2. drawbridges
4. museums

Page 29
Pictures and labels will vary.

Page 34
1. wagons pulled by horses that moved very slowly
2. rode steam trains
3. travel from coast to coast in only one week
4. the conductor, the engineer, the workers who built the tracks, and the workers who kept the trains running well
5. people took shorter train trips because they had to sit up the whole time and could not rest
6. carry people, mail, and goods

Page 35
1. D
2. A
3. C
4. C
Graphic organizers will vary.

Page 36
1. Answers will vary.
2. Answers will vary.
3. Answers will vary.
4. Sample answer: 1. First steam trains carry people in England. 2. Steam trains start running in the United States. 3. People in the United States can travel from coast to coast in one week. 4. People can sleep on trains and take longer trips.
5. Engines are built to make train travel faster.
6. People ride bullet trains that go more than 160 miles per hour.

Page 41
1. D
2. A
3. B
4. A
5. Sample answer: The author says that corn was so important that Native Americans told legends to explain how the plant started, and Corn, Beans, and Squash are in a legend that the author uses as an example.
6. Corn can grow in many places in the world because it can grow in both warm and cold climates.

Page 42
1. crop
2. maize
3. legends
4. stalks
5. kernels
6. cob
7. husks
8. silk

Page 43
1. Menus will vary.
2. Answers will vary.

Page 47
1. B
2. B
3. D
4. A
5. Sample answer: Farmers fed their family with what they grew and raised on their farm. But they had to have some money to buy seeds and clothes and shoes for their family.

6. Sample answer: Children living on farms long ago worked very hard. They got up early to start working. They did things like feed and take care of baby animals and help keep them safe. In the summer and fall they helped pick the crops. In the winter they learned how to cook or build things.

Page 48
1. D
2. B
3. A
4. C
Vocabulary word examples will vary.

Page 49
1. Answers will vary.
2. Sample answer:
   1. Drove a plow through fields; 2. Placed the seeds in the ground in rows; 3. Covered the seeds with soil; 4. Watered the plants; 5. Harvested the crops; 6. Sold the harvest

Page 54
1. Sample answer: Pa took care of his family by always getting food for them to eat, but he moved them around a lot. He even made them move from places where their life was good.
2. Sample answer: Since Mary could no longer see, Pa told Laura that she had to use her own eyes to see things and describe them to Mary.
3. Sample answer: Laura probably wanted to marry someone brave and kind, and Almanzo showed both of these things by his actions.

4. Sample answer: Laura had not really liked moving so much when she was young.
5. Sample answer: Laura became an author because her daughter Rose asked her to write down the stories Laura had told her when she was young about her life as a pioneer.
6. Sample answer: It tells a lot of facts about the life of a person who really lived.

Page 55
1. settle
2. prairie
3. blizzard
4. huddled
5. fever
6. nervous
7. starved
8. mild
9. fiddle

Page 56
1. Answers will vary.
2. Sample answer: Compare (Alike): Winter weather was harsh. Lived in a log house. Contrast (Different): Lived in a forest in Wisconsin; lived on a prairie with no trees in Kansas. Easier to farm in Wisconsin than in Kansas. Land in Kansas was flat and dry; land in Wisconsin was not.

Page 63
1. D
2. A
3. B
4. C
5. B
6. C

Page 64
1. port
2. subway
3. ballet
4. capital
5. Monuments
6. fort
7. Mummies
8. Pyramids
9. supplies
Words in boxes will vary.

Page 65
1. Drawings and labels will vary.
2. Answers will vary.

Page 72
Answers will vary.
1. Sample answer: wrote a book about his adventures
2. Sample answer: Prince Henry; opening a school to teach sailors how to find their way on the open water and by paying for their voyages
3. Sample answer: Jacques Cousteau; wrote books and made films
4. Sample answer: he never reached Asia
5. Sample answer: explorers like Meriwether Lewis and William Clark explored and mapped the Americas, including the United States
6. Sample answer: they made maps of what they were exploring

Page 73
1. route
2. voyages
3. oceans
4. proved
5. faraway
6. films
7. discovered
Vocabulary words and descriptions will vary.

Page 74
1. Answers will vary.
2. Time lines will vary. Sample answer: Title: Explorers in the 1800s and 1900s. Items: early 1800s—Lewis and Clark explore and map much of the United States; 1909—Henson and Peary reach North Pole; 1911—Amundsen reaches South Pole; 1951–Cousteau maps ocean floor and studies sea life; 1953—Hillary and Norgay reach top of Mount Everest; 1961—Gagarin orbits Earth; 1969—Armstrong and Aldrin walk on moon; 1996–Lucid spends 188 days on space station studying Earth.

Page 80
Answers will vary.
1. Sample answer: Charles had to go to college in another state because he was turned down by the University of South Carolina, which was in his home state.
2. Sample answer: Studying at the Naval Academy was harder for Charles than for most of the other students because, besides all the difficult classes and tough military training, he was one of only a few African Americans.
3. Sample answer: When Charles was young, South Carolina's members of Congress would not help him because he was African American. I think they changed how they thought about him after he became famous for flying the space shuttle.

4. Sample answer: Even though around 1964 African Americans had a hard time finding support to get into a college, Charles wrote many letters asking for support from South Carolina's members of Congress.
5. Sample answer: This passage is a biography because it tells a lot of facts about the life of a person who really lived.
6. Sample answer: The author most likely wrote this passage to give details about the life of an African American who overcame many challenges to do what he wanted to do.

Page 81
1. persistence
2. candidate
3. persevered
4. obstacles
5. challenge
6. determined
7. uplifting
Graphic organizers will vary.

Page 82
1. Answers will vary.
2. Answers will vary.

Page 87
1. C
2. B
3. C
4. D
5. The president travels to other countries to represent the United States.

Page 88
1. A
2. C
3. C
4. D
5. C
6. A
7. B
8. D

Page 89
1. Sample answer: Main Idea: A difficult job of the president is to direct the country's relationships with foreign countries. Supporting Details: has the power to make treaties with other countries; can refuse to speak with new foreign governments; can suggest laws that help foreign governments; can act as a world peacemaker
2. Answers will vary.